Vegan Delightful Desert Recipes

34 Fun, Delicious and Easy Desert Recipe's

Teal Kimball

Contents in this book include:

34 Fun, Delicious and Easy Desert Recipe's

This desert book offers 34 mouth-watering vegan dessert recipes that will satisfy any sweet tooth while adhering to a plant-based lifestyle.

For vegan dessert lovers looking to expand their recipe repertoire, this book provides a variety of easy-to-follow and delicious recipes that will impress any dinner guest, Whether you're a seasoned vegan or just starting out, these 34 fun and delectable dessert recipes are perfect for anyone looking to indulge in a guilt-free and cruelty-free treat.

Vegan Banana Bread

Ingredients:
3 ripe bananas, mashed
1/4 cup coconut oil, melted
1/4 cup maple syrup
1 tsp vanilla extract
1 1/2 cups whole wheat flour
1 tsp baking soda
1/2 tsp cinnamon
Pinch of salt

Instructions:

1. Preheat oven to 350°F (175°C) and grease a loaf pan.

2. In a bowl, mix mashed bananas, coconut oil, maple syrup, and vanilla extract.

3. In a separate bowl, combine flour, baking soda, cinnamon, and salt.

4. Gradually add the dry ingredients to the wet ingredients and mix until just combined.

5. Pour the batter into the loaf pan and bake for 50 60 minutes or until a toothpick inserted comes out clean.

6. Let it cool before slicing and serving.

Vegan Whole Wheat Bread

Ingredients:

3 cups whole wheat flour

1 packet (2 1/4 tsp) instant yeast

1 1/2 cups warm water

1 tablespoon maple syrup or agave nectar

1 teaspoon salt

2 tablespoons olive oil

Instructions:

1. In a large bowl, combine the warm water, yeast, and sweetener. Let it sit for 5 10 minutes until it becomes frothy.

2. Add the flour, salt, and olive oil to the yeast mixture. Mix until a rough dough forms.

3. Knead the dough on a floured surface for about 8 10 minutes until smooth and elastic.

4. Shape the dough into a ball and place it in an oiled bowl. Cover with a damp cloth and let it rise for about 1 hour or until doubled in size.

5. Punch down the dough, shape it into a loaf, and place it in a greased loaf pan.

6. Cover and let it rise for another 30 45 minutes. Preheat your oven to 375°F (190°C).

7. Bake the bread for 30 35 minutes until golden brown and hollow sounding when tapped.

8. Let it cool before slicing. Enjoy your homemade vegan whole wheat bread!

Vegan Zucchini Bread

Ingredients:

1 1/2 cups shredded zucchini

1/2 cup unsweetened applesauce

1/2 cup maple syrup or agave nectar

1/4 cup plant based milk

1 teaspoon vanilla extract

2 cups whole wheat flour

1 teaspoon baking powder

1/2 teaspoon baking soda

1/2 teaspoon salt

1 teaspoon ground cinnamon

1/2 teaspoon ground nutmeg

Optional: chopped walnuts, raisins

INSTRUCTIONS:

1. Preheat your oven to 350°F (175°C) and grease a bread loaf pan.

2. In a large bowl, mix together the shredded zucchini, applesauce, maple syrup, plant based milk, and vanilla extract.

3. In a separate bowl, whisk together the flour, baking powder, baking soda, salt, cinnamon, and nutmeg.

4. Gradually add the dry ingredients to the wet ingredients and mix until just combined. Fold in nuts or raisins if desired.

5. Pour the batter into the prepared loaf pan and smooth the top.

6. Bake for 50 60 minutes or until a toothpick inserted into the center comes out clean.

7. Allow the zucchini bread to cool in the pan for 10 minutes before transferring it to a wire rack to cool completely.

Vegan Pumpkin Bread

Ingredients:
1 3/4 cups whole wheat flour
1 teaspoon baking soda
1/2 teaspoon baking powder
1/2 teaspoon salt
1 teaspoon ground cinnamon
1/2 teaspoon ground nutmeg
1/4 teaspoon ground cloves
1 cup pumpkin puree
1/2 cup maple syrup or agave nectar
1/3 cup coconut oil, melted
1/4 cup plant based milk
1 teaspoon vanilla extract
Optional: chopped nuts, pumpkin seeds

Instructions:

1. Preheat the oven to 350°F (175°C) and grease a loaf pan.

2. In a large bowl, whisk together the flour, baking soda, baking powder, salt, and spices.

3. In another bowl, mix the pumpkin puree, maple syrup, coconut oil, plant based milk, and vanilla extract.

4. Gradually add the dry ingredients to the wet ingredients and stir until just combined. Fold in nuts or seeds if desired.

5. Pour the batter into the prepared loaf pan and smooth the top.

6. Bake for 50 60 minutes or until a toothpick inserted in the center comes out clean.

7. Let it cool in the pan for 10 minutes before transferring to a wire rack to cool completely.

Vegan Strawberry Coconut Ice Cream

Ingredients:

2 cups frozen strawberries

1 can full fat coconut milk

1/4 cup maple syrup or agave syrup

1 teaspoon vanilla extract

Instructions:

1. In a blender, combine the frozen strawberries, coconut milk, maple syrup, and vanilla extract.

2. Blend the mixture until smooth and creamy.

3. Transfer the mixture to a container and freeze for at least 4 6 hours or until firm.

4. Allow the ice cream to sit at room temperature for a few minutes before scooping and serving.

5. Enjoy the vegan strawberry coconut ice cream on its own or with your favorite toppings.

Vegan Mint Chocolate Chip Ice Cream

Ingredients:

2 cans full fat coconut milk

1 cup fresh mint leaves

1/2 cup maple syrup or agave syrup

1 teaspoon peppermint extract

1/2 cup dairy free chocolate chips

Instructions:

1. In a saucepan, heat one can of coconut milk with the fresh mint leaves over medium heat. Let it simmer for about 5 10 minutes.

2. Remove the mint leaves and transfer the mixture to a blender. Blend until smooth.

3. In a large bowl, combine the blended mixture with the second can of coconut milk, maple syrup, and peppermint extract. Mix well.

4. Pour the mixture into an ice cream maker and churn according to the manufacturer's instructions.

5. In the last few minutes of churning, add in the dairy free chocolate chips.

6. Transfer the ice cream to a container and freeze for a few hours until firm.

7. Scoop and enjoy the refreshing vegan mint chocolate chip ice cream!

Vegan Peanut Butter Banana Ice Cream

Ingredients:
4 ripe bananas, peeled, sliced, and frozen
1/2 cup creamy peanut butter
1/4 cup nondairy milk (such as almond or coconut)
1 teaspoon vanilla extract
Optional toppings: crushed peanuts, chocolate syrup

Instructions:

1. Place the frozen banana slices, peanut butter, nondairy milk, and vanilla extract in a food processor or blender.

2. Blend the ingredients until smooth and creamy, scraping down the sides as needed.

3. Transfer the mixture to a container and freeze for 1 2 hours for a firmer texture.

4. Serve the vegan peanut butter banana ice cream in bowls, drizzle with chocolate syrup, and sprinkle with crushed peanuts.

5. Indulge in this creamy and delightful vegan dessert!

Vegan Banana Ice Cream

Ingredients:

4 ripe bananas, sliced and frozen

1/4 cup plant based milk (such as almond or coconut milk)

Optional toppings (nuts, chocolate chips, fruit)

Instructions:

1. Place the frozen banana slices and plant based milk in a high speed blender or food processor.

2. Blend until smooth and creamy, scraping down the sides as needed.

3. You may need to pause and stir the mixture a few times to ensure even blending.

4. Once the mixture is smooth and creamy, transfer it to a container and freeze for about 1 2 hours.

5. Scoop the banana ice cream into bowls and add your favorite toppings before serving.

Vegan Mango Sorbet

Ingredients:
2 ripe mangoes, peeled and diced
1/4 cup maple syrup or agave nectar
1/4 cup coconut milk
1 tsp lime juice

Instructions:

1. In a blender, combine the diced mangoes, maple syrup/agave nectar, coconut milk, and lime juice.

2. Blend until smooth.

3. Pour the mixture into a shallow dish and freeze for 4 6 hours, stirring every hour until set.

4. Serve the mango sorbet in bowls and enjoy!

Vegan Blueberry Basil Sorbet

Ingredients:

2 cups fresh or frozen blueberries

1/2 cup fresh basil leaves

1/4 cup agave syrup

1 tsp lemon juice

Instructions:

1. In a blender, combine the blueberries, basil leaves, agave syrup, and lemon juice.

2. Blend until smooth.

3. Pour the mixture into a shallow dish or ice cream maker and freeze for 4 6 hours, stirring every hour if using a dish.

4. Serve the sorbet in bowls with fresh basil leaves as a garnish.

VEGAN CHOCOLATE CAKE

Ingredients:
1 1/2 cups all-purpose flour
1 cup granulated sugar
1/4 cup cocoa powder
1 teaspoon baking powder
1/2 teaspoon baking soda
1/2 teaspoon salt
1 cup nondairy milk (such as almond or soy)
1/3 cup vegetable oil
1 tablespoon apple cider vinegar
1 teaspoon vanilla extract

Instructions:

1. Preheat your oven to 350°F (180°C) and grease a round cake tin.

2. In a large mixing bowl, whisk together the flour, sugar, cocoa powder, baking powder, baking soda, and salt.

3. In a separate bowl, mix the nondairy milk, vegetable oil, apple cider vinegar, and vanilla extract.

4. Pour the wet ingredients into the dry ingredients and mix until well combined.

5. Pour the batter into the prepared cake tin and smooth the top with a spatula.

6. Bake in the preheated oven for 30 35 minutes, or until a toothpick inserted into the center comes out clean.

7. Remove the cake from the oven and let it cool in the tin for 10 minutes before transferring to a wire rack to cool completely.

8. Once the cake is completely cool, you can frost it with your favorite vegan frosting or enjoy it as is!

Vegan Carrot Cake

Ingredients:

2 cups all-purpose flour

1 1/2 teaspoons baking powder

1 teaspoon baking soda

1/2 teaspoon salt

1 teaspoon ground cinnamon

1/2 teaspoon ground nutmeg

1/2 cup vegetable oil

3/4 cup brown sugar

1/2 cup unsweetened applesauce

1 teaspoon vanilla extract

1 1/2 cups grated carrots

1/2 cup chopped walnuts or pecans (optional)

Vegan cream cheese frosting (store bought or homemade)

INSTRUCTIONS:

1. Preheat your oven to 350°F (180°C) and grease a cake tin.

2. In a large bowl, whisk together the flour, baking powder, baking soda, salt, cinnamon, and nutmeg.

3. In another bowl, mix the vegetable oil, brown sugar, applesauce, and vanilla extract.

4. Pour the wet ingredients into the dry ingredients and mix until just combined.

5. Fold in the grated carrots and chopped nuts, if using.

6. Pour the batter into the prepared cake tin and spread it out evenly.

7. Bake for 30 35 minutes, or until a toothpick inserted into the center comes out clean.

8. Once the cake is completely cool, frost it with vegan cream cheese frosting and serve.

Vegan Rose Cardamom Pistachio Cake

Ingredients:

2 cups all-purpose flour

1 cup almond milk

1/2 cup coconut oil

1 cup sugar

1 tsp rose water

1 tsp ground cardamom

1/2 cup shelled pistachios

Instructions:

1. Preheat the oven to 350°F (180°C) and grease a cake pan.

2. In a bowl, mix together the flour, almond milk, coconut oil, sugar, rose water, and ground cardamom until smooth.

3. Fold in the shelled pistachios.

4. Pour the batter into the cake pan and bake for 30 35 minutes or until a toothpick inserted comes out clean.

5. Let the cake cool before serving.

Vegan Peanut Butter Chocolate Bars

Ingredients:

1 cup smooth peanut butter

1/2 cup maple syrup

1/2 cup coconut oil, melted

1 tsp vanilla extract

2 cups rolled oats

1/2 cup dairy free chocolate chips

Instructions:

1. Line an 8x8 inch baking dish with parchment paper.

2. In a saucepan, melt peanut butter, maple syrup, and coconut oil over low heat, stirring until smooth.

3. Remove from heat and stir in vanilla extract.

4. Fold in the rolled oats until well combined.

5. Transfer the mixture to the prepared baking dish and spread evenly.

6. In a small saucepan, melt the chocolate chips and drizzle over the peanut butter mixture.

7. Refrigerate for 2 3 hours until set, then cut into bars and enjoy.

Vegan Apple Crisp

Ingredients:

4 apples, peeled and sliced

1/2 cup rolled oats

1/4 cup almond flour

1/4 cup maple syrup

2 tsp coconut oil

1 tsp cinnamon

Instructions:

1. Preheat oven to 350°F (175°C) and grease a baking dish.

2. Place sliced apples in the baking dish.

3. In a bowl, mix rolled oats, almond flour, maple syrup, coconut oil, and cinnamon.

4. Sprinkle the oat mixture over the apples.

5. Bake for 30 35 minutes or until the topping is golden brown.

6. Serve warm with dairy free vanilla ice cream or whipped coconut cream.

Vegan Mixed Berry Crisp

Ingredients:

3 cups mixed berries (such as blueberries, raspberries, and strawberries)

1/2 cup granulated sugar

1 tablespoon cornstarch

1 cup all-purpose flour

1/2 cup rolled oats

1/2 cup brown sugar

1/2 teaspoon cinnamon

½ cup of oil

Instructions:

1. Preheat your oven to 350°F (180°C).

2. In a bowl, toss the mixed berries with granulated sugar and cornstarch. Place the mixture in a baking dish.

3. In another bowl, combine the flour, oats, brown sugar, and cinnamon. Add the diced butter and mix until the mixture resembles coarse crumbs.

4. Sprinkle the crumb

Vegan Lemon Blueberry Cheesecake Bars

Ingredients:

For the crust:

1 cup almond flour

1/4 cup coconut oil, melted

2 tsp maple syrup

For the filling:

1 1/2 cups raw cashews, soaked overnight

1/4 cup coconut oil, melted

1/4 cup maple syrup

Zest and juice of 1 lemon

1 cup blueberries

Instructions:

1. Preheat the oven to 350°F (180°C) and line a baking dish with parchment paper.

2. In a bowl, mix almond flour, melted coconut oil, and maple syrup to form the crust mixture.

3. Press the crust mixture into the prepared baking dish and bake for 10 12 minutes until lightly golden. Allow it to cool.

4. In a blender, combine soaked cashews, melted coconut oil, maple syrup, lemon zest, and lemon juice. Blend until smooth and creamy.

5. Pour the filling over the cooled crust and spread evenly.

6. Drop blueberries onto the filling and swirl with a knife.

7. Refrigerate the cheesecake bars for at least 4 hours or until set before slicing and serving.

Vegan Matcha Coconut Tarts

Ingredients:

1 cup shredded coconut

1/2 cup coconut cream

2 tsp maple syrup

1 tsp matcha powder

1/2 tsp vanilla extract

Instructions:

1. In a bowl, mix together the shredded coconut, coconut cream, maple syrup, matcha powder, and vanilla extract until well combined.

2. Press the mixture into tart molds or a lined muffin tin.

3. Chill in the refrigerator for at least 1 hour to set.

4. Top with extra shredded coconut or sliced almonds before serving.

Vegan Earl Grey Chocolate Truffles

Ingredients:
1 cup dairy free chocolate chips
1/2 cup coconut cream
2 tsp Earl Grey tea leaves
Cocoa powder for coating

Instructions:

1. In a saucepan, heat the coconut cream and Earl Grey tea leaves until warm. Let it steep for 10 minutes.

2. Strain the coconut cream and heat it again until hot.

3. Pour it over the chocolate chips and mix until smooth.

4. Chill the mixture for 1 2 hours until firm.

5. Roll into balls, coat with cocoa powder, and serve.

Vegan Chocolate Avocado Pie

Ingredients:

For the crust:

1 ½ cups almond flour

⅓ cup maple syrup

3 tsp coconut oil, melted

For the filling:

2 large ripe avocados

½ cup cocoa powder

½ cup maple syrup

½ tsp vanilla extract

Pinch of salt

Optional toppings:

Fresh berries

Shredded coconut

Vegan whipped cream

Instructions:

1: Preheat your oven to 350°F (180°C).

In a bowl, mix almond flour, maple syrup, and melted coconut oil until well combined.

Press the mixture into a pie dish, covering the bottom and sides evenly.

Bake the crust for about 10 12 minutes, and then let it cool.

2. Prepare the filling:

In a food processor, combine avocados, cocoa powder, maple syrup, vanilla extract, and salt.

Blend the mixture until smooth and creamy, scraping down the sides as needed.

3. Assemble the pie:

Pour the avocado chocolate mixture into the cooled crust.

Vegan Lemon Blueberry Pie

Ingredients:

For the crust:

1 ½ cups almond flour

⅓ cup coconut oil, melted

3 tsp maple syrup

For the filling:

1 ½ cups fresh blueberries

1 cup coconut cream

½ cup maple syrup

Zest and juice of 2 lemons

3 tsp cornstarch

Optional toppings:

Lemon slices

Fresh blueberries

Vegan whipped cream

Instructions:

1: Preheat your oven to 350°F (180°C).

In a bowl, combine almond flour, melted coconut oil, and maple syrup until a dough forms.

Press the dough into a pie dish, covering the bottom and sides evenly.

Bake the crust for about 12 15 minutes, then let it cool.

2. Prepare the filling:

In a saucepan, combine blueberries, coconut cream, maple syrup, lemon zest, lemon juice, and cornstarch.

Cook over medium heat, stirring constantly until the mixture thickens.

3. Assemble the pie:

Pour the blueberry filling into the cooled crust.

Vegan Berry Chia Pudding

Ingredients:

1/4 cup chia seeds

1 cup almond milk

1 tsp maple syrup or agave nectar

1/2 tsp vanilla extract

Mixed fresh berries (e.g., strawberries, blueberries, raspberries)

Instructions:

1. In a bowl, mix chia seeds, almond milk, maple syrup/agave nectar, and vanilla extract.

2. Let it sit in the refrigerator for at least 2 hours or overnight to thicken.

3. Layer the chia pudding with fresh mixed berries in serving glasses or jars.

4. Garnish with more berries on top and serve chilled.

Vegan Coconut Rice Pudding

Ingredients:

1 cup cooked white rice

1 can coconut milk

1/4 cup maple syrup or agave nectar

1 ripe mango, diced

Toasted coconut flakes for garnish

Instructions:

1. In a saucepan, combine the cooked rice, coconut milk, and maple syrup/ agave nectar. Cook over low heat until the mixture thickens.

2. Remove from heat and let it cool slightly.

3. Stir in the diced mango.

4. Transfer the rice pudding to serving bowls, garnish with toasted coconut flakes, and chill before serving.

Vegan Grilled Pineapple with Coconut Cream

Ingredients:

1 ripe pineapple, peeled, cored, and sliced into rings

1 can full fat coconut milk, chilled overnight

2 tsp maple syrup or agave nectar

1 tsp vanilla extract

Pinch of cinnamon (optional)

Instructions:

1. Preheat a grill or grill pan over medium high heat.

2. Grill the pineapple slices for about 2 3 minutes per side until grill marks form.

3. While the pineapple is grilling, open the chilled coconut milk can and scoop out the thick coconut cream that has risen to the top.

4. Whip the coconut cream with maple syrup/agave nectar and vanilla extract until fluffy.

5. Serve the grilled pineapple with a dollop of coconut cream on top. Sprinkle with a pinch of cinnamon if desired.

Vegan Mixed Fruit Salad with Citrus Mint Dressing

Ingredients:

Assorted fresh fruits (such as strawberries, kiwi, oranges, grapes, pineapple, etc.), chopped

Zest and juice of 1 orange

Zest and juice of 1 lemon

2 tsp maple syrup or agave nectar

Fresh mint leaves, chopped

Instructions:

1. In a large bowl, combine the chopped fruits.

2. In a separate bowl, whisk together the orange zest, orange juice, lemon zest, lemon juice, maple syrup/agave nectar, and chopped mint leaves.

3. Pour the citrus mint dressing over the mixed fruits and toss gently to coat.

4. Chill the fruit salad in the refrigerator for at least 30 minutes before serving.

Vegan Lemon Lavender Shortbread Cookies

Ingredients:
1 cup flour
1/2 cup vegan butter
1/4 cup powdered sugar
1 tsp dried lavender
Zest of 1 lemon

Instructions:

1. Preheat the oven to 350°F (180°C) and line a baking sheet with parchment paper.

2. In a bowl, cream together the vegan butter and powdered sugar until smooth.

3. Add the flour, dried lavender, and lemon zest to the bowl and mix until a dough forms.

4. Roll out the dough on a floured surface and use cookie cutters to cut out shapes.

5. Place the cookies on the baking sheet and bake for 10 12 minutes or until the edges are slightly golden.

6. Let the cookies cool before serving.

Vegan Peanut Butter Cookies

Ingredients:

1 cup all-purpose flour

1/2 teaspoon baking soda

1/2 teaspoon salt

1/2 cup creamy peanut butter

1/2 cup coconut oil, melted

1/2 cup brown sugar

1/4 cup granulated sugar

1 teaspoon vanilla extract

Instructions:

1. Preheat your oven to 350°F (180°C) and line a baking sheet with parchment paper.

2. In a medium sized bowl, whisk together the flour, baking soda, and salt.

3. In a large bowl, mix the peanut butter, melted coconut oil, brown sugar, granulated sugar, and vanilla extract until smooth.

4. Gradually add the dry ingredients into the wet ingredients, stirring until well combined.

5. Scoop out tablespoon sized portions of dough and roll them into balls. Place them on the prepared baking sheet.

6. Using a fork, gently press down on each cookie to create a cross pattern.

7. Bake for 10 12 minutes, or until the cookies are set and golden.

8. Allow the cookies to cool on the baking sheet for a few minutes before transferring them to a wire rack to cool completely.

Vegan Oatmeal Raisin Cookies

Ingredients:

1 cup rolled oats

3/4 cup all-purpose flour

1/2 teaspoon baking soda

1/2 teaspoon ground cinnamon

1/4 teaspoon salt

1/3 cup coconut oil, melted

1/3 cup maple syrup

1 teaspoon vanilla extract

1/2 cup raisins

Instructions:

1. Preheat your oven to 350°F (180°C) and line a baking sheet with parchment paper.

2. In a mixing bowl, combine the rolled oats, flour, baking soda, cinnamon, and salt.

3. In a separate bowl, mix together the melted coconut oil, maple syrup, and vanilla extract.

4. Gradually add the wet ingredients to the dry ingredients, stirring until a dough forms.

5. Fold in the raisins until evenly distributed.

6. Using a cookie scoop or spoon, drop tablespoon sized portions of dough onto the prepared baking sheet.

7. Flatten each cookie slightly with the back of a spoon.

8. Bake for 12 15 minutes, or until the edges are golden brown.

9. Let the cookies cool on the baking sheet for a few minutes before transferring them to a wire rack to cool completely.

Vegan Almond Butter Cookies

Ingredients:

1 cup almond butter

1/2 cup coconut sugar

1 flax egg (1 tablespoon ground flaxseed + 3 tablespoons water)

1 teaspoon vanilla extract

1/2 teaspoon baking soda

1/4 teaspoon salt

1/3 cup dairy free chocolate chips (optional)

Instructions:

1. Preheat your oven to 350°F (180°C) and line a baking sheet with parchment paper.

2. In a mixing bowl, prepare the flax egg by mixing together the ground flaxseed and water. Let it sit for a few minutes to thicken.

3. Add the almond butter, coconut sugar, vanilla extract, baking soda, and salt to the bowl with the flax egg. Mix until well combined.

4. Fold in the dairy free chocolate chips if using.

5. Using a cookie scoop, drop spoonful's of dough onto the prepared baking sheet.

6. Flatten each cookie with a fork or your fingers.

7. Bake for 10 12 minutes, until the edges are set.

8. Let the cookies cool on the baking sheet for a few minutes before transferring them to a wire rack to cool completely.

Vegan Chocolate Avocado Mousse

Ingredients:
2 ripe avocados
1/4 cup cocoa powder
1/4 cup maple syrup
1 tsp vanilla extract
Pinch of salt

Instructions:

1. Scoop out the flesh from the avocados and place in a food processor.
2. Add cocoa powder, maple syrup, vanilla extract, and salt.
3. Blend until smooth and creamy.
4. Serve in small bowls and refrigerate for at least 30 minutes before serving.
5. Optional: Top with chopped nuts or berries before serving.

Vegan Lemon Blueberry Muffins

Ingredients:

1 1/2 cups all-purpose flour

1/2 cup granulated sugar

2 tsp baking powder

1/4 tsp salt

1/2 cup unsweetened applesauce

1/4 cup plant based milk (such as almond or soy milk)

1/4 cup melted coconut oil

1 tsp vanilla extract

Zest of 1 lemon

1 cup fresh or frozen blueberries

INSTRUCTIONS:

1. Preheat the oven to 375°F (190°C) and line a muffin tin with paper liners.

2. In a large mixing bowl, whisk together the flour, sugar, baking powder, and salt.

3. In a separate bowl, combine the applesauce, plant based milk, melted coconut oil, vanilla extract, and lemon zest.

4. Pour the wet ingredients into the dry ingredients and stir until just combined. Be careful not to over mix.

5. Gently fold in the blueberries.

6. Spoon the batter into the prepared muffin tin, filling each cup about 3/4 full.

7. Bake for 20 25 minutes or until a toothpick inserted into the center of a muffin comes out clean.

8. Allow the muffins to cool in the tin for a few minutes before transferring them to a wire rack to cool completely.

Vegan Chocolate Cupcakes

Ingredients:

1 1/2 cups all-purpose flour

1 cup granulated sugar

1/4 cup cocoa powder

1 tsp baking soda

1/2 tsp salt

1 cup water

1/3 cup vegetable oil

1 tsp white or apple cider vinegar

1 tsp vanilla extract

Instructions:

1. Preheat your oven to 350°F (180°C) and line a cupcake tray with paper liners.

2. In a large mixing bowl, whisk together the flour, sugar, cocoa powder, baking soda, and salt.

3. Add the water, vegetable oil, vinegar, and vanilla extract to the dry ingredients. Mix until just combined, being careful not to over mix.

4. Fill each cupcake liner about two thirds full with the batter.

5. Bake the cupcakes in the preheated oven for 18 20 minutes or until a toothpick inserted into the center comes out clean.

6. Remove the cupcakes from the oven and let them cool in the tray for a few minutes before transferring them to a wire rack to cool completely.

7. Once the cupcakes are completely cooled, you can frost them with your favorite vegan frosting or enjoy them plain!

vegan Lavender Lemon Cupcakes

Ingredients:
For the cupcakes:
1 1/2 cups all-purpose flour
1 cup granulated sugar
1 tsp baking powder
1/2 tsp baking soda
1/4 tsp salt
1 cup almond milk
1/3 cup vegetable oil
1 tsp apple cider vinegar
Zest of 1 lemon
1 tsp dried lavender buds
For the frosting:
1/2 cup vegan butter, softened

2 cups powdered sugar

2 tsp almond milk

1 tsp lemon extract

Dried lavender buds for garnish

Instructions:

1. Preheat your oven to 350°F (175°C) and line a cupcake tin with cupcake liners.

2. In a large mixing bowl, combine the flour, sugar, baking powder, baking soda, and salt. Mix well.

3. In a separate bowl, whisk together the almond milk, vegetable oil, apple cider vinegar, lemon zest, and dried lavender buds.

4. Pour the wet ingredients into the dry ingredients and mix until just combined. Be careful not to over mix.

5. Divide the batter evenly among the cupcake liners, filling each about two thirds full.

6. Bake in the preheated oven for 18 20 minutes or until a toothpick inserted into the center of a cupcake comes out clean.

7. Remove the cupcakes from the oven and allow them to cool completely on a wire rack.

8. While the cupcakes are cooling, make the frosting. In a mixing bowl, beat the vegan butter until creamy. Gradually add the powdered sugar, almond milk, and lemon extract, and beat until smooth and creamy.

9. Pipe or spread the frosting onto the cooled cupcakes.

10. Garnish each cupcake with a sprinkle of dried lavender buds.

Vegan Matcha Green Tea Cupcakes

Ingredients:
For the cupcakes:
1 1/2 cups all-purpose flour
1 cup granulated sugar
1 tsp baking powder
1/2 tsp baking soda
1/4 tsp salt
1 cup almond milk
1/3 cup vegetable oil
1 tsp apple cider vinegar
2 tsp matcha green tea powder
For the frosting:
1/2 cup vegan butter, softened
2 cups powdered sugar

2 tsp almond milk

1 tsp vanilla extract

Additional matcha green tea powder for dusting

Instructions:

1. Preheat your oven to 350°F (175°C) and line a cupcake tin with cupcake liners.

2. In a large mixing bowl, combine the flour, sugar, baking powder, baking soda, salt, and matcha green tea powder. Mix well.

3. In a separate bowl, whisk together the almond milk, vegetable oil, apple cider vinegar.

4. Pour the wet ingredients into the dry ingredients and mix until just combined.

5. Divide the batter evenly among the cupcake liners, filling each about two thirds full.

6. Bake in the preheated oven for 18 20 minutes or until a toothpick inserted into the center of a cupcake comes out clean.

7. Remove the cupcakes from the oven and allow them to cool completely on a wire rack.

8. Meanwhile, prepare the frosting. In a mixing bowl, beat the vegan butter until creamy. Gradually add the powdered sugar, almond milk, and vanilla extract, and beat until smooth and creamy.

9. Pipe or spread the frosting onto the cooled cupcakes.

10. Lightly dust the top of each cupcake with a sprinkle of matcha green tea powder.

These vegan dessert recipes are sure to satisfy your sweet cravings and provide a cool treat for any occasion. Enjoy!

About the author

Teal J. Kimball, Born in 1988 is a Spiritual Researcher & Discoverer of many Spiritual teachings, Findings & Healings. Educating through a Place Where Science Meets Spirituality & You Can Find All Sorts Of Soulful Nourishment, Including Health Food Benefits, Quantum Mechanics Energy, Science, Horticulture & Agriculture Teachings.

Website www.TealKimball.com

About the Author

Teal J. Kimball, Born in 1988 is a Spiritual Researcher & Discoverer of many Spiritual teachings, Findings & Healings. Educating through a Place Where Science Meets Spirituality & You Can Find All Sorts Of Soulful Nourishment, Including Health Food Benefits, Quantum Mechanics Energy, Science, Horticulture & Agriculture Teachings.

Read more at www.TealKimball.com.

www.ingramcontent.com/pod-product-compliance
Lightning Source LLC
Chambersburg PA
CBHW050602160726
48003CB00003B/1013